This book belongs to

John & Col Selmo

Oct '95

Walt Disney® VOLUME 7

BIRDS AND TREES, FLOWERS AND BEES

WALT DISNEY FUN-TO-LEARN LIBRARY

ISBN 0-9619525-8-X
Advance Publishers Inc., P.O. Box 2607, Winter Park, FL. 32790
Printed in the United States of America
0987654321

"What a beautiful day!" cried Snow White when she opened the front door of the dwarfs' cottage. "I've been waiting for a day like this so we could explore the woods."

"Good idea, Princess," said Doc. "We'll have a picnic."

Grumpy grumbled that picnics were for people who had nothing better to do, but he helped Snow White pack the basket, and off they all went.

Outside the cottage, the first thing
they saw was a pair of red-breasted
robins flying off with worms in their beaks.

"Look, the father and mother birds are going to feed the babies in
the nest," said Snow White. "When baby robins hatch out of their eggs,
they cannot fly. Their busy parents have to keep feeding them until they
can fly off and get their own food."

The male robin perched by his nest and sang while his mate took her
turn feeding the hungry little robins.

"Caw! Caw! Caw!" called out a
bird from a tree above them.

"What an ugly sound!" said Grumpy, clapping his hands over
his ears.

"It's a big black crow with raggedy wings," said Snow White.
"Hundreds of them make their untidy nests in tall trees."

"Crows are a noisy bunch," declared Doc, "but they are clever. Not
even a scarecrow can scare them."

"Caw! Caw! Caw!" screeched a handsome blue jay as it flew high
above the woodland path. It was as noisy as the crow, and just as daring.

"Tock-tock-tock!"

"What's that?" asked Bashful.

"It must be a woodpecker," said Snow White. "It's pecking holes in that tree, looking for insects to eat."

"That tapping is so loud, you'd think it would wake Sleepy up," said Doc, looking at Sleepy curled up under the tree.

"Nothing wakes up Sleepy," said Grumpy, who was trying to shake Sleepy awake.

As they walked on through the woods, they came to a
crowd of twittering sparrows.

Happy liked the little birds with their black caps. He pulled
a slice of bread out of his pocket and scattered bread crumbs
for them. The sparrows seemed to enjoy the treat.

Suddenly, they were surrounded by a greedy flock of pigeons.
"They sure aren't afraid of us," said Sleepy with a yawn.
"Of course they aren't," said Snow White, "and neither is my lovely pet dove." She stroked its soft feathers.
"Coo, coo," said the dove.

"Snow White," said Doc, as he passed an old maple tree. "Look into this tree hole."

Snow White looked, and saw a row of baby owls, or owlets. The fluffy babies opened their large eyes and blinked, sleepily.

Owls sleep all day when most birds are awake. At night, they open their soft, downy wings. They swoop down silently to catch rats and mice in their sharp claws.

Above a clearing in the woods, a hawk hung high in the sky. Suddenly, it dove down. Its sharp eyes had spotted a rabbit running across the grass.

But the rabbit was too quick for the hawk, and it sneaked down its hole before the hawk could catch it.

A few birds hunt animals or other birds for food. Most birds eat insects or seeds.

Chickadees are like tiny acrobats as they hunt for insects to eat. When Dopey saw some of them hanging upside down on a tree branch, he thought he'd join them.

And down fell Dopey— into a soft pile of leaves.

Up flew a bright red bird, surprised by Dopey's fall. It was a male cardinal, who was looking for acorns to eat.

"*Tsit!*" he said angrily, as he stared down at Dopey.

A tiny bird flew by Snow White's hand.

"You look like a brilliant, shimmering jewel," said Snow White. "I know that you're a bird, but your wings move so fast I can hardly see them."

The hummingbird was sipping a sweet liquid called nectar from a honeysuckle flower, using its pointed beak and long tongue to poke deep inside.

Sneezy tried to bury his nose in the flower, but his nose was too big. So he sneezed instead.

"Look there," said Snow White with a smile. "I think I see someone inside that tree."

Sure enough, there was Bashful playing hide-and-seek in a hollow in an old willow tree.

All kinds of animals lived in or near the dwarfs' favorite tree.

Some orioles had made their nests in the top branches.

A baby raccoon fished with its mother in a nearby pond.

A family of foxes were playing around a hollow log near their den in the roots of the tree.

A chipmunk skittered across the log on the way to its hole in the tree trunk.

And Doc pushed Dopey on the swing he had made from an old piece of rope.

The woods are full of different trees. They are beautiful to look at, at any time of year.

In spring, the flowers on cherry trees and dogwood trees make them look as if they were covered with pink and white snow.

In summer, mighty oak trees shade us from the sun.

In autumn, the red colors of maple tree leaves make the tree look as if it were on fire.

In winter, when other trees are bare, the fir trees and spruces and pines remain a deep, dark green.

"Trees are the biggest of all plants," said Snow White. "But they, too, start from little seeds. The seeds of the apple tree are found deep inside the apple.

"Some trees, such as walnut and almond trees, grow nuts.

"And pine trees grow pine cones. Inside the cones are little, wing-shaped seeds."

As the seedling grows and grows into a tree, its branches sprout twigs and leaves.

Its trunk becomes covered with tough bark.

In the spring, buds unfold and flowers appear.

In the autumn, seeds from the fruits and nuts and cones fall to the ground and new seedlings start to grow.

Trees can live to be very, very tall and very, very old—much older than the oldest person!

Snow White and the dwarfs walked on until they came to a field full of flowers.

"How beautiful," said Snow White. "Let's pick some and bring them back to the cottage.

"Here's a white daisy, and here's a yellow one. Did you know that the word *daisy* means 'day's eye'? Many daisies close up their petals, or their 'eyes,' when the sun goes down!"

"And here's a dandelion," said Doc. "Look how light and fluffy its seeds are! They blow away with a puff of air and take root where they land." He puffed at a ball of dandelion seeds and watched a little cloud of them float away.

Happy made a daisy chain out of the dainty white and yellow flowers.

"What is making that wonderful smell?" asked Happy.
"Those are wild roses," said Snow White.
"*Yeowtch!*" yelled Grumpy. "They bit me!"
"Oh, Grumpy, roses don't bite," said Snow White. "But they do have thorns. You must be careful when you pick them."

"Snow White, look what I've found!" called Sneezy.
"It's a seedpod full of poppy seeds," Snow White answered.
Sneezy turned the seedpod upside down, and out poured
its tiny black seeds. "*Aa-CHOO!*" he sneezed.

"Well done, Sneezy," said Doc. "Now that you have spread
the poppy seeds on the ground, next spring the bees might have
poppy flowers to visit along with
this sweet clover."

"What is this wonderful blue flower?" asked Happy.

"That's a morning glory," said Snow White.

"It's mighty pretty," said Bashful. "It looks just like the blue color in your dress."

Snow White smiled, and Bashful blushed.

"Look how the morning glory winds itself around the tree," said Snow White. "Ivy does the same thing. Sometimes ivy clings so tightly that it chokes the tree."

"Stay away!" Grumpy warned Dopey, who was just about to pick some red-and-green leaves. "That's poison ivy! You'll get an itch if you touch it!"

At the edge of the flower field was the dwarfs' little garden. Busily the dwarfs started gathering good things to eat. They picked carrots and cucumbers, lettuce and celery, and strawberries and raspberries—all these foods and many others are plants.

Doc opened the picnic basket and laid out their lunch.

"Here's bread for our sandwiches," he said.

"Bread is made from the ground-up seeds of a grass called wheat," said Snow White, pulling up a stalk of wild wheat from the edge of the garden.

Everybody enjoyed the picnic—especially the ants.

The ants marched, single file, back to their nest under the tree stump. Some of the ants were carrying crumbs of bread almost as big as themselves.

Ants live together in little ant towns.

If you had magic eyes, this is what you'd see inside the ant town.

Tiny tunnels lead down into little rooms.

In the deepest chamber of all, the huge queen ant is laying eggs. Worker ants carry the eggs into the hatching rooms.

In the hatching rooms, the eggs are being cared for by the worker ants. They clean them and carry them from place to place to keep them warm. Soon the eggs will hatch into fat little grubs. In time, these grubs will change into adult ants.

Soldier ants stand guard at the entrance of the anthill, ready to fight off enemies and to build up crumbling walls.

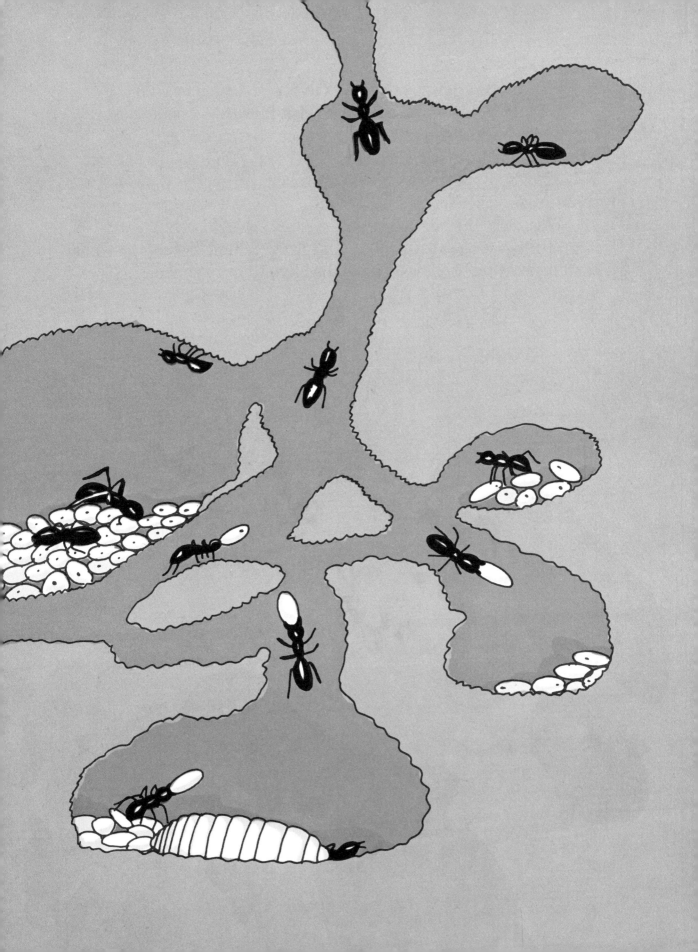

A bee buzzed right by Grumpy's nose and landed on a flower.

"Why do bees —*aa-choo*—like to visit flowers?" asked Sneezy.

"The honeybee sips sweet nectar from the flower," said Snow White. "The bee's furry sides get covered with the flower's yellow pollen. Pollen holds lots of tiny seeds the bee 'plants' in another flower. From these seeds, other flowers will grow."

"What does the bee do with the nectar?" asked Bashful.

"It brings it back to its hive," said Snow White. "Honeybees build their hives in tree hollows. Inside the hive, they make thousands of tiny cells.

"The queen bee lays her eggs in them. From the eggs, little grubs hatch. When they grow up, they will become bees. The adult bees feed the little grubs with the honey they make from nectar and pollen."

"Busy bees!" said Happy.

"Huh," said Grumpy. "They have a nasty sting, too."

"But only if you scare them," said Snow White.

"Flutter by, butterfly," said Snow White, as the gaily colored creature settled on her hand.

"Can you believe that the butterfly starts life as a lowly caterpillar?" she asked.

The mother butterfly lays her eggs in a shady spot. The eggs hatch into caterpillars.

The caterpillars eat and eat until they are ready to grow up. Then they make silky coats around themselves, called cocoons.

Inside its cocoon, the caterpillar slowly changes its shape. And one day, it breaks out of its cocoon as a beautiful butterfly.

Moths, which fly mostly at night, go through the same wonderful change.

A tiny, spotted ladybug beetle rested gently on Snow White's hand.

"Did you know there are millions of beetles in the world?" she asked. "Some beetles are pests that eat up plants we grow for food. But the ladybug beetle eats thousands of little insects that suck the juices out of plants. Ladybugs save the lives of the plants by eating the tiny insects, and this is one of the reasons people love the little red ladybugs.

"Ladybug, ladybug, fly away home," said Snow White, as she blew gently on her hand.

The ladybug opened her black-and-white spotted wings and flew away.

The spider in a nearby bush had caught one little brown beetle in its sticky web.

Beetles may be large or small, striped or spotted, colored or plain. Some beetles have horns or helmets. All have antennae, or feelers, which help them find out what is going on around them. And most have hard, shiny covers that protect the soft wings underneath.

Snow White and the dwarfs stopped to rest beside a pond.
Suddenly, a beautiful insect with shiny wings darted past Doc's nose.
"That's a dragonfly," said Snow White. "But, of course, it isn't really
a dragon. And it isn't dangerous—except to some other insects. It eats
lots of biting, stinging insects, like mosquitoes and gnats."

Other insects were busy near the pond—and on it.

"Look, there's a giant water bug, paddling with its legs like little oars," said Snow White, "Do you see the huge eyes it has?

"And there's a water strider—it walks on the water on those long, thin legs."

"And there is Dopey, falling in the water!" said Grumpy.

Doc put the picnic cloth around poor Dopey to dry him off.

"Listen," said Snow White. She had noticed the sounds of chirps all around them. "Can you hear the songs of the crickets and the grasshoppers? They rub their wings or their knees together to make many different kinds of noises."

"Maybe it's their way of talking to each other," said Doc. "They sure do make a lot of noise, especially when the night is warm."

Crickets are small, brown creatures that often live in people's houses.

Grasshoppers are bigger insects, with long legs and neatly folded wings. Their green color matches the grass or the leaves where they live.

Loud chirping came from a nearby branch. Dopey leaned forward to get a better look. Suddenly, a huge grasshopper sprang into the air on its long, strong legs. Dopey was so frightened, he ran away!

"Well," said Doc, "I guess it's time to go home." He winked at
Snow White.

"Oh, I do want to stay out long enough to see the fireflies," Snow
White replied. "You go on ahead. I'm sure Grumpy won't mind keeping
me company." And she winked back at Doc.

So, Grumpy stayed with Snow White while the other dwarfs went back to the cottage. "I'm getting hungry," he grumbled. "Those fireflies had better show up."

Soon, tiny lights began to flicker.

"It's like magic," gasped Snow White.

"Aw, it's just the male fireflies blinking their lights on and off. They're signaling to each other and to the female glowworms."

The glowworms lay on the ground and twinkled back at their flying friends.

"Grumpy, I'm glad you said you'd wait with me," said Snow White. "This is a beautiful sight."

"*Hmmph!*" Grumpy grumped. "Fireflies are for sissies."

When Snow White and Grumpy opened the door of the cottage, Grumpy gasped.

"Surprise!" shouted all the dwarfs.

"It's your birthday, Grumpy, and we've been planning this party for you all day," explained Snow White.

Grumpy was so touched by the idea of his friends giving him a party that he forgot for a moment to be gruff. "Oh, thank you," he said, looking around the cottage at all the decorations.

"Well, Grumpy," said Snow White, "aren't you glad now you stayed out with me to watch the fireflies?"

"Aw, I couldn't leave you out alone in the dark."

Snow White laughed. "That's all right, Grumpy," she said. "Let me say it for you—this is the perfect end to a perfect day!"